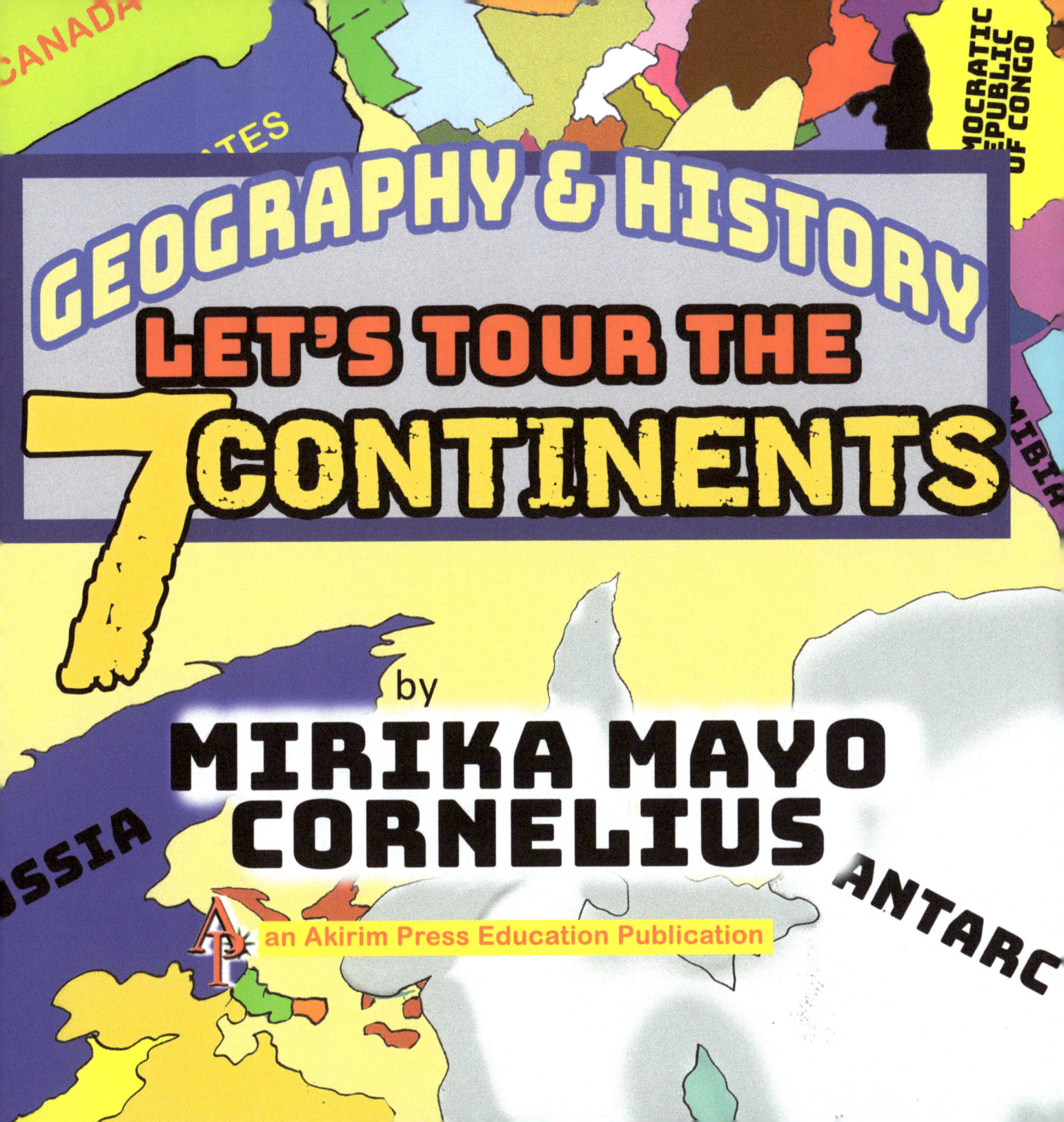

Geography & History
Let's Tour the 7 Continents

Copyright © Mirika Mayo Cornelius, September 2023
mirikacornelius.com

No part of this publication my be reproduced, stored in any way, shape or form, or transmitted in any form or by any means, orally/verbally, digital, drawn or written, without the written permission of the author or publisher. For information about permissions, contact akirimpress@gmail.com.

This is a work of children's educational non-fiction. Names, characters, places and incidents are either products of the author's imagination or are used fictitiously. Any resemblance to actual events or locales or persons, living or dead, is entirely coincidental.

All rights reserved, including the rights of reproduction in whole or in part in any form.

Copyright © Mirika Mayo Cornelius, September 2023
ISBN: 978-1-946870-18-6

An Akirim Press Publishing
Book Cover and Illustrations by Mirika Mayo Cornelius
www.akirimpress.com

ACKNOWLEDGEMENTS

I thank
God the Father, Jesus and the Holy Ghost for making all of what I do possible. I also acknowledge my family, great educators and those who support great, truthful education.

GET MORE FUN, EDUCATIONAL BOOKS AT AKIRIM PRESS EDUCATION!

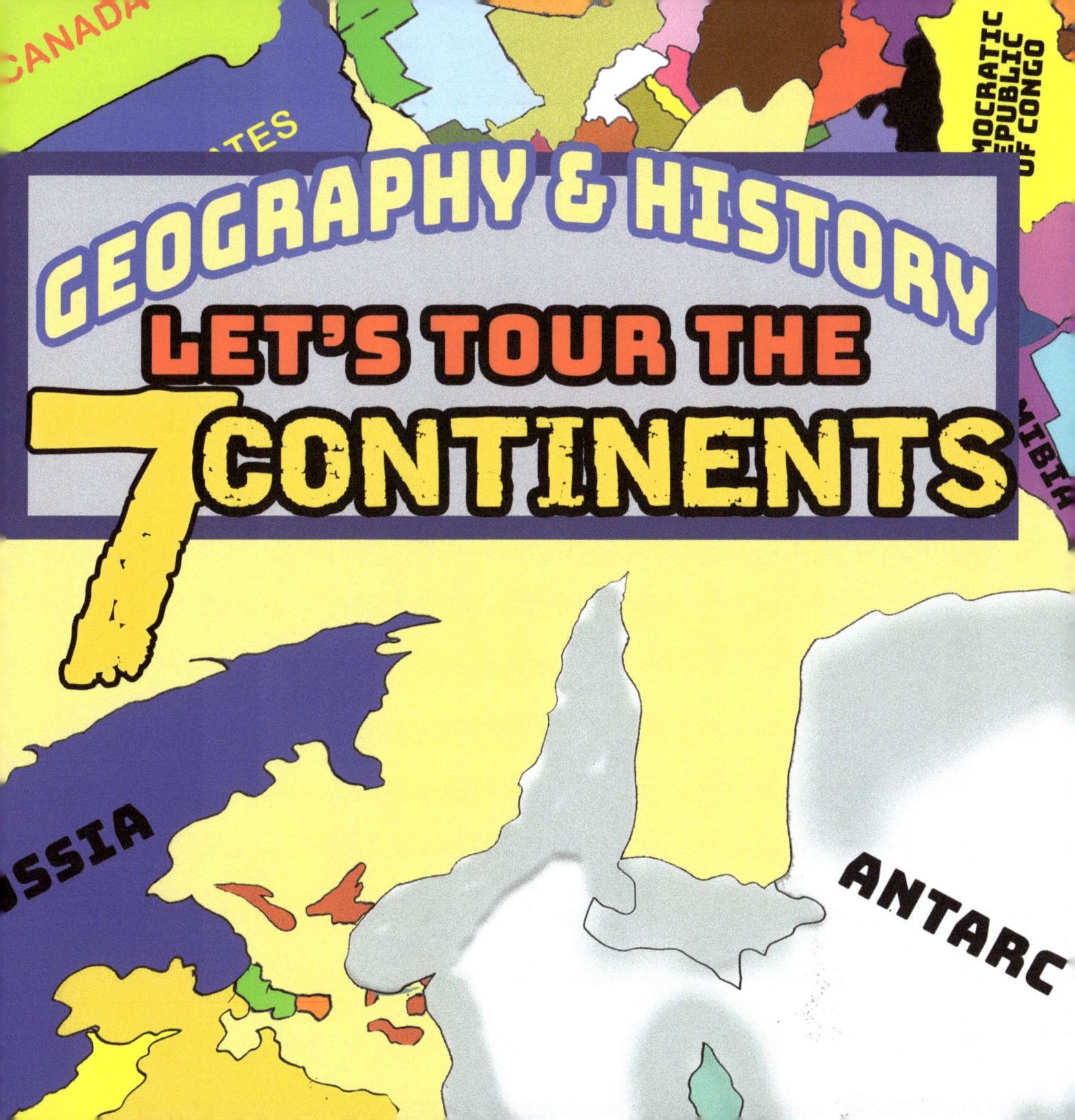

THE CONTINENT
AFRICA

FACTS ABOUT AFRICA

Africa is home to some of the world's largest, fiercest and most beautiful land animals. Giraffes, lions, cheetahs and even elephants are some of the wild animals that live on this continent. Africa is even home to one of the most venomous snakes called the Black Mamba.

Because Africa is the cradle of humanity, or where life is thought to have originated, one of the world's greatest discoveries came from the people of this continent. That discovery is the making of fire!

Some of the world's greatest man-made wonders are found in Egypt and Sudan, and those wonders are the pyramids. Also, a natural wonder in Africa is the Nile River, and it's the longest river in the whole world! It runs from Egypt, through Ethiopia and all the way to the Democratic Republic of Congo.

Finally, the country of South Africa was the home of the country's first democratically elected president - Nelson Mandela. He was a civil rights leader in his country and fighter against the system called apartheid.

THE CONTINENT
ASIA

FACTS ABOUT ASIA

Asia is home to a variety of wild anmials such as the snow leopard, king cobra and even elephants. Even the Giant panda lives on this continent, sharing the land mass with antelopes and rhinoceros!

Asia is the largest continent on the earth, and it stretches from the north of Africa all the way to the north of North America! The Himalaya mountain range is in Asia, and Mount Everest is part of the Himalayas. Mount Everest is the highest of all mountains in the world!

Did you know that there's a country in Asia that has the same name as a bird? That country is Turkey! The tallest waterfall in Turkey is the Tortum Waterfall, and the Koprulu Canyon is also in Turkey. It's a canyon and national park!

Finally, the country of China is on the Asian continent, and China has the largest population of people on earth. India, which is also on the Asian continent, has the second largest population on the globe.

THE CONTINENT
ANTARCTICA

FACTS ABOUT ANTARCTICA

Antarctica is the coldest continent on the globe, but it isn't just the coldest on earth. It has the highest elevation of any continent on earth! Did you know Antarctica is also super dry? It's true! Even though it is icy and surrounded by water, Antarctica is considered a cold desert, so instead of miles and miles of dirt, there miles of sheets of ice that don't even melt!

If you ever travel to Antarctica, some animals you may see are polar bears, whales and penguins. There are even elephant seals! Finding food at the right time is very important to all land animals on this continent.

Another thing about Antarctica is that there are icebergs everywhere. The icebergs float in the water, and they are massive in size. As a matter of fact, Antarctica has the most icebergs on the entire planet.

Finally, Antarctica doesn't have a huge population of people who are indigenous to the land, and because of that, there are no countries on this continent. Though people live here at times, Antartica is not their permanent home. They leave!

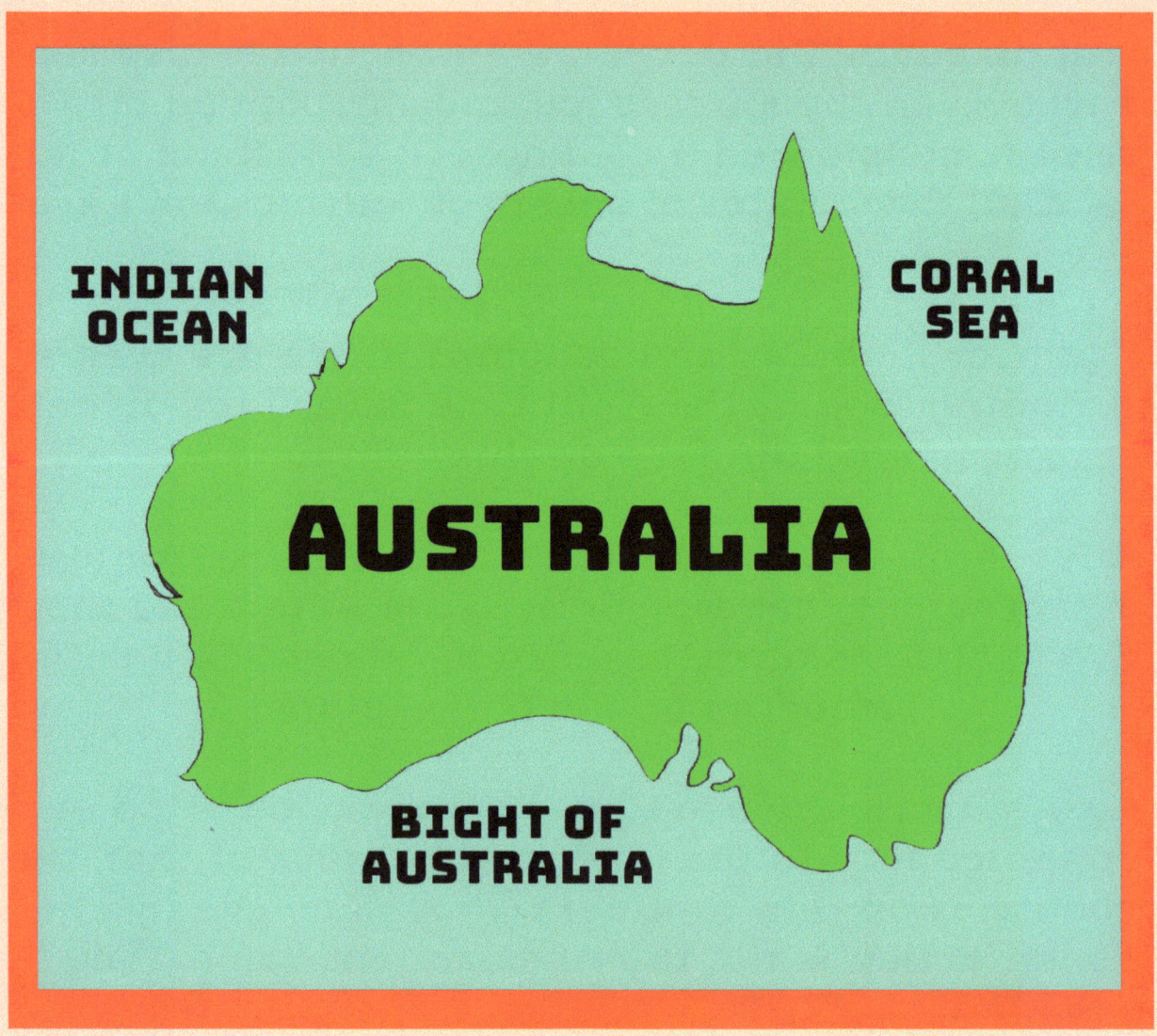

FACTS ABOUT AUSTRALIA

Australia is home to some very interesting animals like the Tasmanian devil and kangaroos. Koalas, parrots and cockatoos also live on this continent that is also a country at the same time!

The original, indigenous people of Australia are called Aborigines. The continent was all theirs for thousands of years until it was colonized by other people, and this led to an Aboriginal population decrease over time. However, Australia is still their home!

An Australian Aborginal man named Neville Bonner was the first Aboriginal to serve in federal parliament of Australia. He was a leader in civil rights and fairness for Aboriginal people.

Finally, one of the natural wonders of the world is in Australia, and that is the Great Barrier Reef. The Great Barrier Reef is home to thousands of fish! Australia also has a natural wonder called the Wave Rock, and it looks just like a high ocean wave where surfers surf!

FACTS ABOUT EUROPE

Europe is home to some of the world's most dangerous land animals like the wolverine and the European viper! The continent is also home to smaller, less dangerous animals like the red squirrel and the Eurasian beaver.

Did you know that a part of the Asian countries Russia and Turkey are also a part of Europe? They are! These countries are called transcontinental because they are in both.

Some natural wonders in Europe include the Dolomite Mountains in Italy and the river canyon called the Verdon Gorge that is located in the country of France! A man-made wonder of the world is also in France, and it's called the Eiffel Tower, famous because a long time ago, it used to be the tallest structure build in the world until 1930.

Finally in Europe, a German man named Johann Gutenberg invented the world's first printing press, and an Afro-European man born in London, England of the United Kingdom named Samuel Coleridge-Taylor became a world renowed classcal musician and composer!

THE CONTINENT
NORTH AMERICA

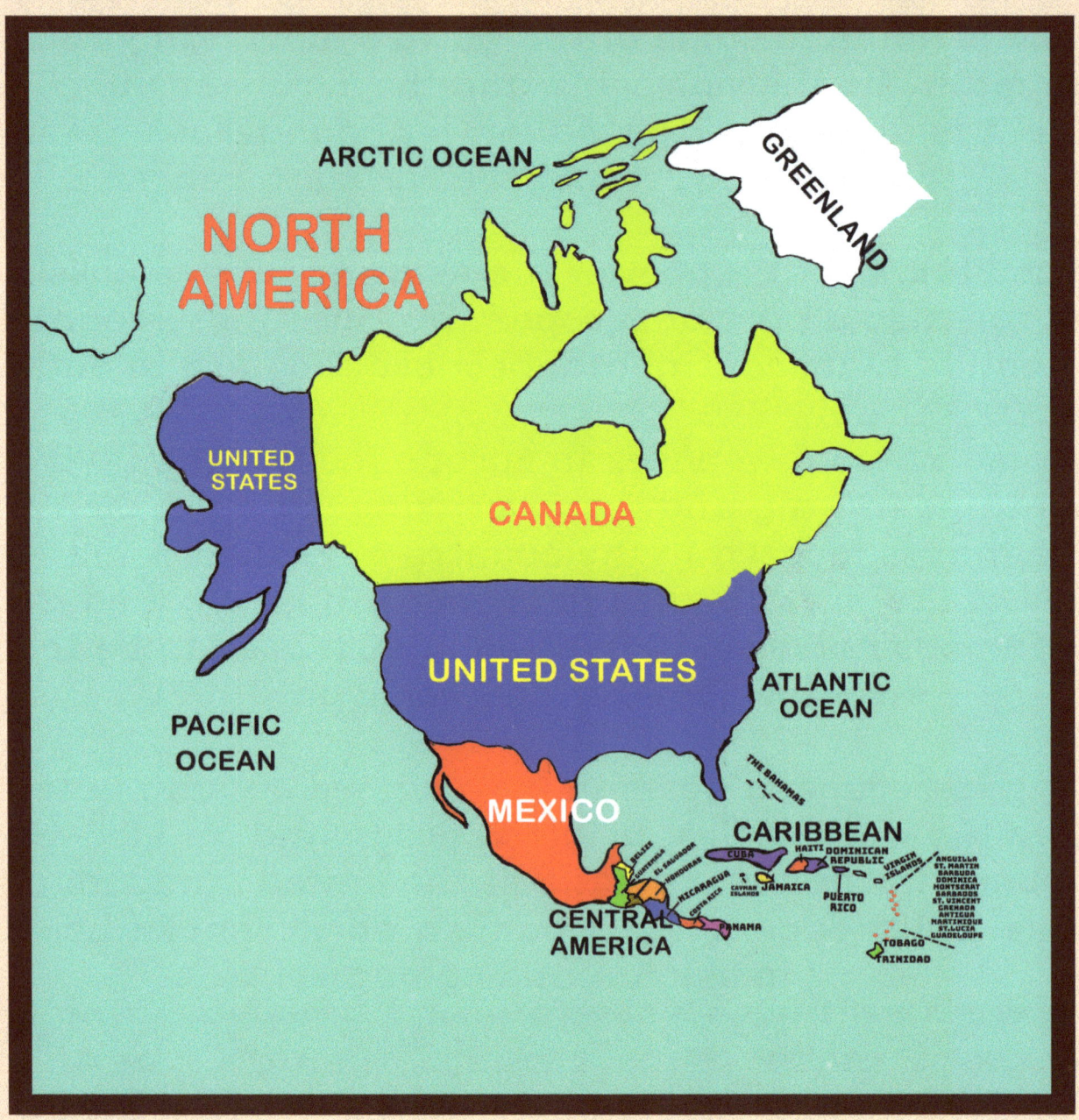

FACTS ABOUT NORTH AMERICA

Bears, alligators, and red foxes are wild animals that live on this continent. North America is also home to bison, deer and even big horn sheep!

Some insects that are found on this continent are hardly ever seen, like the giant lacewing. There are more common insects that start off as one thing and end up another, like the caterpillar that turns into a butterfly!

Also, North America is home to many different inventions! One of those inventions is the traffic light, invented by an African American man from the United States named Garrett Morgan, and that traffic light is used worldwide!

Finally, North America has some of the most beautiful natural wonders in the world, such as the Grand Canyon and White Sands Desert in the United States, Hopewell Rocks in Canada, the Great Blue Hole in Belize, Agua Azul Waterfalls in Mexico, Green Grotto Caves in Jamaica and Ilulissat Icefjord in Greenland.

THE CONTINENT
SOUTH AMERICA

FACTS ABOUT SOUTH AMERICA

Anacondas, spider monkeys, and toucans are wild animals that live on this continent. South America is also home to the sloth, pygmy marmosets, and even the king vulture!

One of the world's greatest inventions came from an Afro-Surinamese man who was born in the South American country of Suriname. His name was Jan Matzeliger. After moving to the United States, he became an Afro-Surinamese American and invented the shoe laster! Now hundreds of pairs of shoes can be made in hours instead of weeks!

Also, South America is home to the world's most vast rainforest, called the Amazon rainforest! Most of that rainforest is in the country of Brazil, but it spans into other contries of South America as well.

Finally, South America has some of the most interesting insects that live in its Amazon rainforest, and one of them is the largest centipede in the entire world called the Scolopendra gigantea, or the Peruvian Giant Yellow-Leg Centipede. It's venomous!

THERE ARE SEVEN
CONTINENTS

AFRICA

ASIA

ANTARCTICA

AUSTRALIA

EUROPE

NORTH AMERICA

SOUTH AMERICA

LET'S TAKE CARE OF OUR LANDS

CLEAN UP

DON'T LITTER

PLANT TREES AND FLOWERS

RECYCLE

DECREASE AIR POLLUTION

CONSERVE WATER

For more learning fun, get your educational books from Akirim Press Education at

akirimpress.com/akirim-press-education

www.ingramcontent.com/pod-product-compliance
Lightning Source LLC
Chambersburg PA
CBHW041232240426
43673CB00010B/314